DOING IT!

RH

this book is dedicated without anxiety to all my influences and to every writer who has ever written and to every aspiring writer I say

"Let no one ever steal your joy!"

DOING IT!

writing the perfect poem

john b. lee

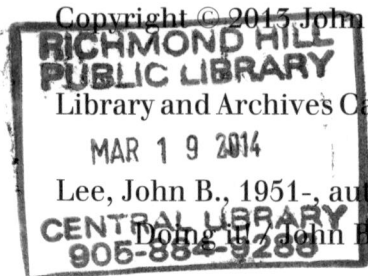

Copyright © 2013 John B. Lee

Library and Archives Canada Cataloguing in Publication

Lee, John B., 1951-, author
    Doing it / John B. Lee.

ISBN 978-0-88753-521-5 (pbk.)

1. Poetry--Authorship. I. Title.

PN1059.A9L44 2013   808.1   C2013-903832-9

Design & Layout by Jason Rankin
Cover image by Marty Gervais

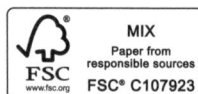

MIX
Paper from
responsible sources
FSC
www.fsc.org   FSC® C107923

Black Moss
EST. 1969 **Press**

Published by Black Moss Press at 2450 Byng Road,
Windsor, Ontario, N8W 3E8. Canada. Black Moss books
are distributed in Canada and the U.S. by LitDistCo. All
orders should be directed there.

Black Moss would like to acknowledge the generous
financial support from both the Canada Council of the
Arts and the Ontario Arts Council.

ONTARIO ARTS COUNCIL
CONSEIL DES ARTS DE L'ONTARIO
50 YEARS OF ONTARIO GOVERNMENT SUPPORT OF THE ARTS
50 ANS DE SOUTIEN DU GOUVERNEMENT DE L'ONTARIO AUX ARTS

Canada Council   Conseil des arts
for the Arts   du Canada

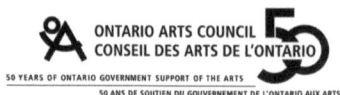

Table of Contents

part i
DOING IT!

part ii
And Furthermore!

DOING IT!

DOING IT! Writing the perfect poem—the state of continual becoming

"I like a state of continual becoming, with a goal in front and not behind."
George Bernard Shaw

If you aspire, as do I, to write a perfect poem, then you also know that this is an impossible task. And it is this very impossibility that gives meaning and purpose to inspiration.

I'd far rather have it said of me that I write poems, than have it said that I am a poet. Never mind the prodigious output, the list of accomplishments, the accolades,

7

awards, and high-praise. All of these are fine and good, but I still delight in the doing. I chase the feeling when the writing is going well. I write because I love to write. In the words of Paul Celan, "I trust that the poem is solitary and on its way."

First—be a reader; be a reader, first: learning what language can do

Recently I came into possession of two very precious family artifacts. I remember them well from my early childhood. They'd sat as though lost in the midst of dozens of other books on the shelf of the hallway bookcase located just outside of the door of my childhood farmhouse bedroom. These little blue-bound objects are books filled with pen-and-ink drawings accompanied by Chinese pictographic writing. I loved everything about them. The delicate bone-clasp fasteners, the thin and slightly yellowed rice-paper pages captured and sewn in small gatherings, the indigo illustrations, and the intricate vertical logograms, fascinated me as a preliterate child. I longed to unlock their inner mystery. When I cracked the covers of these books that I had not seen for forty years, I rediscovered where, as a four-year-old preschooler, I'd printed my name on the inside of the end boards. I suppose I was simply taking possession. Perhaps I was dreaming that I'd written these books, for I'd also scribbled on several of the pages leaving evidence of my earliest attempts at writing. The graphite record of the movement of my hand had scribed a line in its wake like the small spiked waves of a wind-stirred sea. To this day, I prefer a pencil to all other tools of my craft.

I still don't know the meaning of the content of the writing. Neither my preliterate scribbling nor the Chinese pictographs is comprehensible to me. I have a secret wish that these pictographs might be illustrated poems. I suspect they are not. One day I will seek out and find someone who might tell me what they are. That desire to learn to read and the impulse to write remain deeply connected in me. Reading and writing are essential correlatives. I do not see great value in disentangling the two. However, if someone were to hold my feet to the fire, I would say, "First and foremost be a reader." If you want to be a writer, read widely, read well, and read as a writer must read. Otherwise how might you learn what language can do?

In the interests of self-editing, of learning your craft, of learning how to begin a poem, of learning where the poem should end, of learning how to make the poem sing, the aspiring writer needs first to attend to the best in the writing of others. In other words, the apprentice writer needs to be a reader. The aspiring writer in learning the craft must develop a refinement of taste, a reliability of judgment, a breadth of knowledge, a depth of understanding, a perspicacity of perception, a perspicuity of expression, quality of experience, clarity of thought, and a love of language and of what language can do in a master's hands. Reading inspires writing. Reading fires the imagination. Northrop Frye for his part called for an educated imagination.

When I was a very young writer, I met Margaret Avison. She was serving as writer-in-residence at University of Western Ontario where I was a third-year student working on an undergraduate degree in English. I'd been writing poetry for many years. Although my mother and sister had read some of my work, this was the first occasion when I actually had the courage to show my work to a stranger. I'd brought a manuscript for her consideration. She invited me to sit down and before she would allow me to show her any of my work she asked, "Who do you read?"

I gushed about Coleridge. I enthused about Dylan Thomas. I told her how much I loved the poetry of Irving Layton. I spoke of Emily Dickinson, of Catullus, of Elliot and Frost. I confessed to the purchase of a book of Byron's poetry that I had found in a bookstore in Chatham, Ontario when I was sixteen. I championed Michael Ondaatje's recent masterpiece *The Collected Works of Billy the Kid*. I showed her dogeared copy of David McFadden's *Letters from the Earth to the Earth* I'd been carrying around for weeks. I told her about my recent discovery of Atwood's *Journals of Susanna Moodie*. I hadn't mentioned having read Avison's poems. I feared she might ask me about them. And though I didn't realize it at first, I'd passed a test. And now, as a sometime mentor to young writers, and as a frequent instructor in creative writing, I always begin with this same question. "Who do you read?" The answer winnows the grain from the chaff.

Margaret Avison might have put it this way: "If you aspire to be a writer, and you aren't a reader, stop wasting my time!"

An Outpouring

"Time, solitude, toil are the main old-time requisites ... give way to every beckoning to write ... a gift for outpouring."
    Carl Sandburg in a letter to aspiring writer Martha Dodd

Books are not born in libraries. Writers are. Inspired by the poetry of others, my journey began. I wanted to do what they were doing. There were no creative writing courses available to me. I had no actual guidance. My earliest mentors were ink-and-paper with my breath in the words. As a reader/re-creator I had hit upon a way of learning my craft without benefit of formal instruction. Of course my reading apprenticeship was dependent upon the quality of schooling. Because the requirements of education put such heavy demands on my time, school was mostly an obstacle to writing. I may have enjoyed learning in school, but I enjoyed my self-directed apprenticeship even more.

For me, writing began as an outpouring. I read and reread, read and reread the work of masters. I copied out their poems. The lyric of the song "Nowhere Man" by John Lennon of The Beatles was the first piece of writing I ever copied and I did so spontaneously without being required by a teacher. I remember my mother coming into my room and finding Lennon's lyric in my typewriter. She asked, "Did you write that?" I hesitated. I considered a lie and then told her the truth. I had not written it, though I certainly wished I had.

I started writing partly because I loved the act of writing even more than the results of writing. I saw the Beatles on television and I started writing. I was twelve years old. I wanted to be one of the Beatles. But I was too young, and those jobs were taken. I started to write also because I wanted to do something to get their attention. I started to write because I wanted my mother's praise and my father's approval. I secretly felt the presence of my own budding talent. Somewhere deep inside I knew I was on the right path. The path I was born to.

I wasn't working on homework, I was flipping through a poetry anthology. I was reading at random. I was seeking inspiration. I developed a private method I called 'blurring'. This technique involved deliberate misreading of individual words and entire lines of poetry. In this I found a means of leaping into an opening. I was seeking the state of mind where I might first begin and then succeed in stimulating an outpouring of words.

It would be a long time before I would write my first keeper. That is to say, it would be a long time before I wrote the first poem that remained worthy of my own attention long after the heat of inspiration had cooled. I spent years writing through the garbage, attending to the sharp eye of the after-thinker, the self-doubter, the inner editor whose voice I heard in my head crying out, "That's awful. You can do better than that. Keep this, learn from its shortcomings, acknowledge its glorious failures, but don't ever show anyone. Not now. Not ever."

Somehow I knew the absolute necessity to quiet that naysaying voice when I was seeking to trip the switch in the mind and the body that would allow words to simply flow onto the page. Coincidentally, the aforementioned song, "Nowhere Man," came as a result of Lennon surrendering to the silence. He had spent days trying to force the muse without success. Finally, he surrendered. He quit trying. He gave up the effort and went about his daily tasks. Then suddenly, the floodgates opened and the song came rushing out.

I learned to be present when the poems wanted out. I learned to give in to the impulse to write. To catch things in flight. To surrender to the desire to write. I wrote in the evening. I wrote in the morning. I wrote during lunch break at school. I wrote in detention. I wrote on the big table in the high-school library. I wrote quietly, secretly, and furtively. While others snoozed, I wrote in the postprandial hours of high noon on the farm in the summer. I wrote in the field, at the barn, and in the house. I wrote during every stolen moment. By writing, I learned to write. By reading others, I learned to recognize the important features of a well-wrought poem. By reading my own work, I learned to recognize those moments when I too was hitting upon the best words in the best order. I developed reliable ways of learning how to begin. My overheated imagination was fired by the same hormones that changed my body when puberty struck, so too the muses visited. I drew twin desires from the inner wells of Eros.

Ninety year old American poet Stanley Kunitz, in conversation with the author of the book *The Wild Braid: A Poet Reflects on a Century in the Garden*, said, "So much of the creative life has its source in the erotic." He also said, "Desire is one of the strongest words in the language."

When you write, give in. Surrender to the outpouring. The first draft need not be the best draft, but it more often than not has the most energy. The writer needs to learn to harness that energy, to shape it, to find the best poem in the midst of the mucky mess. It's essential to learn how to begin. And then one learns where to begin, and where to end, and what to remove along the way. Winnowing the dross to find the grain. Culling the grain to find the better grain. Selecting the best grain from the better, seeking the essential grain, the grain that is the poem, and in this most thriving seed — the wild oat that thrills the field.

How to begin—meaning 'where' to begin

I belong to a writing group in London. The other members of the group are all well established, articulate, courteous, and most importantly helpful. Once a month we get together at a member's home to read and critique each other's work. I always vet recent work. I try my very best to make certain to bring something written the morning of the day we meet. I like to read something fresh, something with the blush of creation still present in the wet of the ink. We gather at seven in the evening. We chat, eat, drink, laugh, jest, share enthusiasms, discuss literary events and one another's recent writing accomplishments, and then we workshop everyone's writing.

I always have two caveats when I am considering someone else's work. The first caution I give myself involves the conviction that I could be wrong. Ever careful in expressing my suggestions, I am rarely hesitant. My primary concern is always the improvement of the work. And I am firmly convinced that all final decisions are always entirely those of the author.

When it comes to my own work, I listen carefully to every comment. I measure, weigh, and consider. However, I rarely make changes then and there. Of course, I correct the spelling and the grammar and all errors in fact and every foolish inconsistency in voice that mar the work. In writing, God is in the details. I pay heed to every single jot and tittle, every space and every scrap of punctuation. I do, however, remember what has been said, and when I get home and on the following day or two, I reconsider all suggestions and it is then that I decide what to do. Workshops are only valuable when the person making the suggestion is being helpful, and when the writer has the backbone and inner resolve to hold the line when the line needs to be held.

At our workshop in June, I brought a poem I'd written a few days before. I had been in Niagara Falls on Friday. Written a poem called "Wirewalker," on Saturday morning. Driven to Ottawa Monday evening and on Tuesday read the poem three times, once at the Ottawa Public Library, once at the American Embassy, and once to a roomful of invited guests at the home of the Assistant to the American Ambassador. On every occasion the poem felt great, right, finished. Each audience listened closely, responded enthusiastically, and praised the poem freely. I arrived home on Wednesday afternoon. Thursday morning I drove to London for a meeting with my cousin Steve, drove to Ridgetown to visit my mother, and then finally I drove back to London for our monthly poetry workshop. Needless to say, I had not written a new poem since Saturday morning. I brought "Wirewalker," a poem I'd already read in public three times. I was confident that the poem was a good one and I was pretty secure in the fact that no changes would be needed.

I was wrong. Although everyone responded in a positive way to the poem, almost everyone argued against the opening lines. I resisted the criticism. I quarreled in favour of the lines. I argued that they established point of view. I opined that they affirmed my absolutely necessary presence in the poem. I presented the argument that the lines were essential. I was firmly convinced when I left the meeting that I would hold my ground and keep the lines intact. I sat down the following day. Read the poem. Removed the lines. I realized in that instant that the poem was considerably improved by the change.

"Wirewalker" originally began:

> We watched him
> from the safety
> of a secret location
> as he set out
> on the cable—walking
> over Niagara Falls …

The opening without those lines became:

> he set out
> on the cable—walking
> over Niagara Falls

The poem wanted me out of the way. The poem wanted the wirewalker alone. In my mind's eye, I still see my son and I concealed in a secret location with a perfect vantage point. We are in the original experience. But we are not in the poem. We are present only as invisible witnesses. Our attention is fixed, and the reader's attention is fixed where it belongs, on the wirewalker. The lines "We watched him/ from the safety/ of a secret location" may be how the original poem began, but the lines "he set out/ on the cable—walking/ over Niagara Falls," is where the true poem begins.

How to end—where to end

It has often been said of my work, that I have very strong endings to my poems. It is for others to say whether this is true. I leave it to you to decide. That said, I would argue that the best endings in poems are open endings. I endorse endings that open out, and then fold the reader backwards into the poem, not as summations of meaning, nor as conclusions to the poem, but rather as an invitation to re-read the poem from the beginning. These are the best sort of endings. If a poem may be compared to a river, then a poem like a river begins at the source and ends at the mouth. I would argue that the source of the river is also present in the rain, the melting snow, the rills and rushes, the ditches and streams, the unseen aquifers and subterranean water-rich stones that feed the source. What begins before the beginning? Where is the water that brings the river into being? Surely we can imagine its whereabouts. And the mouth empties into and becomes the lake, the sea, and the ocean. Though it vanishes into the larger waters of the bay, it is still there. It is present on the surface and in the deeps. Equally evaporate. Equally blue. So the poem like the river begins before it begins and continues on after its last line is spoken. For the poet, the question is not only how to end the poem, but also where to end the poem. However seductive and elegant this metaphor, the comparison between poems and rivers, the poem must have a closing line.

I recently wrote a poem called, "Her Dark Secret." The poem is a about seeing several emerald wing damselflies laying eggs in a forest glade. The first draft of the poem ended with a series of lines I liked and did not want to lose. Meanwhile, as I read and reread the poem I'd written, I realized that the poem ended with a line located almost in the middle of the poem. I gave myself three choices. Lose the lines entirely. Preserve them for use in another poem. Or fold them into the poem so the poem ends where it should end, with the best line as an ending.

The end I decided upon, or rather the ending the best version of the poem insisted upon:

> it drinks
> the light
> and   shines

The first draft of the poems goes on from there:

> ... at the brave conclusion of desire
> drinks the light
> and   shines
> as it is with the afterthought
> of all incandescent things
> the burning image
> of a lucid dream
> the luminous hallucination
> of a bright line
> all sleep-limned fires
> of the resting mind
> illusionary starswirl
> milting the twin fringes of creation
> from the soaked rim
> of this living river
> its deep interior
> somewhere in the aquifers
> also somewhere in the lake

Not a bad ending, but the other ending is far better.

Here is the first revision.

> at the brave conclusion of desire
> the burning image
> of a lucid dream
> the luminous hallucination
> of a bright line
> (all sleep-limned fires
> of the resting mind
> illusionary starswirl)*
> milting the twin fringes of creation
> from the soaked rim
> of this living river
> its deep interior
> elsewhere in the aquifers
> elsewhere in the lake
> as it is with
> incandescent things
> it drinks
> the light
> and   shines

Many years ago I wrote a poem called, "The Art of Walking Backwards." Though I remained steadfast in my confidence that it was a good poem, I was never truly satisfied with the final lines. I was quite certain of the quality of the opening of the poem. I kept it as an unpublished pretender, waiting in the queue for two years. Then one day, the last line came to me as in

*these three lines were removed from the final version

a dream. Quite a simple poem, it remains one of my personal favourites. And no one need know that the poems opening sixteen lines took ten minutes to write and the closing four lines took nearly three years. I think they were worth the wait.

The Art of Walking Backwards

You thought you understood
the art of walking backwards.

The way the ground turns to air
at the cliff edge.

The way stones feel
against the heel.

The way the rock face
might slam the spine against a jut.

The way window glass
shatters around you
in a dangerous puzzle of cutting reflections.

The way the doorway stays in its joists
or a tree clings shivering to its roots.

The way thin ice gives over deep water
or the swamp sucks you in slowly
like a dropped stone.

One more step
and you will be beyond the verge
free falling
with gulls in the canyon.

The middle bit—learning what to remove and what to leave— getting it right!

At the same writing workshop where I listened to my fellow writers concerning the opening to the poem "Wirewalker," I also took advice regarding the details in the middle of the poem. The poem as read in Ottawa went like this:

> We watched him
> from the safety
> of a secret location
> as he set out
> on the cable—walking
> over Niagara Falls
> as though balanced on a thread
> in his electric orange raiment
> like a brilliant spider
> on a spinneret
> a lovely incandescent
> gardengus
> this Wallenda
> a third generation daredevil ...

In addition to taking strong exception to the opening, one member, my good friend John Tyndall, who had not protested the opening, pointed out that the spinneret is part of the body of the spider and as such is not the silk, but rather the source of silk. He also corrected the spelling of third generation by suggesting the insertion of a hyphen between the two words. Everyone loved the word "gardengus." Where did you find that word? What a wonderful word! I found it surfing the web. It is a species of spider that is brilliant orange. And from my vantage, Wallenda appeared to be entirely brilliant orange. The following day, my friend informed me that the word "gardengus" was actually a moniker used by someone on the web, and that the spider was called a Marbled Orbweaver.

Thank goodness for John Tyndall. Now the poem reads:

> he set out
> on the cable—walking
> over Niagara Falls
> as though balanced on a thread
> in his electric-orange raiment
> like a brilliant spider
> on a silk
> a lovely incandescent
> Marbled Orbweaver
> this Wallenda
> a third-generation daredevil ...

Editing a poem is simply a matter of making improvements. Perfecting the detail.

Refining the language. Shaping the words. Finding the best and most luminous final version. Authentic. Energetic. Just the right thing for the moment.

What's in a Name—giving a title to a poem

"the title comes last ..."
Tennessee Williams

The primary purpose in giving a poem a title is practical. A title makes a poem easy to find. And if the poet does not give the poem a title, surely someone else will. More often than not the poem with no title takes on the mantle of the first line as its title in the index or table of contents of an anthology. Sometimes that first line replaces the title. This is certainly the case in the most famous English language poem in history. More commonly known by its first line, "Twas the Night Before Christmas," (more recently "The Night Before Christmas"), the author's title for that particular poem is "A Visit from Saint Nicholas."

Some poets resist giving titles to their poems. This is most especially true of imagist poets. American poet e. e. cummings for his part resisted giving titles to individual poems. In his book *110 selected poems*, only two poems are given titles. The remaining poems are referred to in the table of contents using the first line. My favourite example of a poem by cummings for which this strategy goes awry is the poem appearing on page four. In the table of contents this poem is referred to as "in Just—". However, I have found it in many anthologies where the anthologist simply gave the poem a title of his choosing. I have seen it variously referred to as "In Just Spring," "Spring," "Balloon Man," and etc.. Not having given the poem a title gives permission to the editors of anthologies to simply make up a title that satisfies the need to identify the poem in print and to find it in the table of contents. This arbitrary ycleption does not always serve the poem well. On one occasion, I found the poem with its intended title, that is to say, the title sometimes given the poem by cummings. In its original form, it is a three-part poem. The first section of the poem has often been published in isolation. The title for the poem in three parts is, "Chansons Innocentes." This title provides a brilliant counterpoint to the deceptive simplicity of the surface meaning of the poem. This French phrase translates into English as "innocent songs," and it hints at being an allusion to William Blake's masterful suite of poems, *Songs of Innocence and of Experience*. The filter of cummings' title "Chansons Innocentes," highlights the theme of innocence and experience and ultimately the theme of loss of innocence. And when one reads and re-reads the poem as illuminated by this theme it becomes increasingly obvious that this is not a poem to gloss. Indeed, when one reads the poem inspired by the notion of loss of innocence the final image of the "goat-footed/ balloonMan" is ominous and gothic and eerie. One lingers longer and sees the presence of Pan, god of spring. One cannot miss then, the goat as an archetypal creature signifying lust. And given cummings' companion poems in the three part poem, one has the presence of Satan, the cloven-hoofed fallen angel of Biblical times and of post-Biblical popular culture. The Halloween Lucifer, horned, red (or in this case green) is something of a caricature or a melodramatic figure from the cinema of the mind. If you doubt this, you only need read a few lines from part two of "Chansons Innocentes," to confirm the suspicion that there is something evil lurking both on the surface and beneath the surface of this first poem about spring, and in the joyful departure of boys and of girls abandoning their childish games of youth. In part two cummings writes, "...for she knows the devil ooch/the devil outch/the devil/ach the great/green/ dancing/devil/devil//devil/devil/ wheeEEE. And as if to hammer home the bright and ineluctable connection between the goatfooted balloonMan and the devil, the two poems respectively end on the homophonic wee and wheeEEE.

Interestingly, Irving Layton in his book *The Gucci Bag* chose not to print the title of each poem on the page where the poem appears. Rather than that, he chose to site the titles in the table of content. Leonard Cohen places the image of a razor blade at the top of the page where the poems begin in his book *The Energy of Slaves*. These strategies reveal options to fixing the poem without a title on the same page.

I have given frequent talks on the nature of titles. On those occasions I have clearly stated that there need be no obvious connection between the title and the content of the poem. This statement came back to haunt me when I attended a poetry reading and a major Canadian poet said, "John B. Lee taught me that titles don't have to have anything to do with the poem. I found this liberating. So here is a poem, and the title is essentially meaningless. Thanks John." I blushed. Not embarrassed by the praise, but slightly embarrassed to have been so broadly misquoted and so dramatically and publicly misinterpreted. I was happy to have been a liberating influence. I was not happy to have given birth to this disconnection.

On another occasion when I was giving my talk on titles, a publisher changed the focus from meaning to marketing. In fact, that publisher for whom I have the greatest respect, changed the title of an anthology I was editing for his literary press from my chosen title *Let Light Try All the Doors*, to his title *Bonjour Burgundy*. He actually appreciated the beauty of my title, but he said he could not sell the book. I acquiesced without a struggle because of my profound respect for his judgment. I've never truly liked his title, but I certainly appreciate the descriptive quality of his choice. In that poetry is outside of the marketplace and has no stall in the agora of the village, I rarely give a thought to marketing when I chose a title for an individual poem or book of poems. My guiding principle involves the nature of the poem. I name the poem according to the squawk and the squall of the infant in my hands. Three very recent poems of mine have the following titles: "Watching Two Cormorants floating on ice in the lake in late January," "Burning a Hole in Heaven/ Bones on the Moon," and

"Wirewalker." Note the trailing off of proper nouns in the first, the metaphoric counterpoint in the second, and the purely descriptive single noun neologism in the portmanteau word of the third. So, for me choosing a title involves what's available, what it means and how that meaning might illuminate the reader's experience of the poem. In "Wirewalker," I wanted simply to name the poem and to identify the central character in the poem. In "Watching Two Cormorants floating on ice in the lake in late January," I am identifying the point of view and the object of attention of the protagonist. The poem's title gives a sense of fading into the background from the foreground. The background is included, but diminished. In "Burning a Hole in Heaven/Bones on the Moon," the title has two parallel and equally powerful images, but the sequence is essential to understanding that what comes first must come first. And it begs the question, "why?" And the poem answers the questions posed by the reliably curious and questing reader.

Here are some illustrative examples of titles and suggestions as to how they introduce and thereby connect naming of content to the meaning of content.

>Llareggub (Dylan Thomas' original title for Under Milkwood)

Titles that have become part of our culture:

>Babbitt
>Pollyanna
>Quixotic based on Don Quixote

Catch 22*
1984**

Titles that sound great, but which have no known or certain meaning in the mind of most readers:

Waiting for Godot
Wuthering Heights
Sonnets from the Portugese
Far from the Madding Crowd
The Moon is a Sixpence***

Various Titles considered for works:

Gone with the Wind: — Pansy, Tote the Weary Land, Tomorrow is Another Day, Jettison, Milestone, Baa! Baa! Black Sheep.

Hard Times: According to Cocker, Prove it, Stubborn Things, Mr. Grandgrind's Facts, The Grindstone, Two and Two Are Four, Something Tangible, Our Hardheaded Friend, Rust and Dust, Simple Arithmetic, A Matter of Calculation, A Mere Question of Figures, The Grandgrind Philosophy, Fact, Hard-Headed Grandgrind,

*Catch 22 was originally called Catch 14 then Catch 18
**1984 was published in 1948 and the title was created by simply flipping the last two numbers to create a 'futuristic-sounding" title far enough in the future to be evocative
***Somerset Maugham said of this title, "People tell me it's a good title but they don't know what it means. To me it means reaching for the moon and missing the sixpence at one's feet."

Hard Heads and Soft Hearts, Heads and Tails, and Black and White.

The Great Gatsby: Trimalchio in West Egg, Gold-hatted Gatsby, and The High-Bouncing Lover.

A Moveable Feast: The Eye and The Ear, To Write It Truly, Love Is Hunger, It Is Different in the Ring, and The Paris Nobody Knows. His widow Mary, found the title in a letter written by Hemingway in 1950: "If you are lucky enough to live in Paris as a young man, then wherever you go for the rest of your life, it stays with you, for Paris is a moveable feast."

Up The Down Staircase: The Staircase Never Seems to Rust, From a Teacher's Wastebasket, Hi Teach!, Please Do Not Erase, The Paper World of Sylvia Barrett, And Gladly Teche, and Don't Shoot Until You See the Pupils.

"The Rhyme of the Ancient Mairner." would not have taken so well if it had been called "The Old Sailor."

1. Simply Naming

David Copperfield
Lolita
Madame Bovary
The Bible
Moby Dick

2. Evoking or Describing 'content'

> Women in Love
> Sons and Lovers
> Portrait of the Artist as a Young Man
> Lives of Girls and Women
> The World According to Garp

3. Being Metaphorical

> All Quiet on the Western Front
> Catcher in the Rye
> Sophie's Choice
> Of Human Bondage
> To Kill a Mockingbird
> Great Expectations
> Fifth Business

4. Being Deliberately Cryptic

> Do Androids Dream of Electric Sheep
> For Those Who Hunt The Wounded Down

5. Titles as Allusions

> The Sound and the Fury
> Ulysses
> For Whom the Bell Tolls
> By Grand Central Station I Sat Down and Wept

6. How the meaning can change by changing even the smallest of words:

Anne of Green Gables becomes Anne in Green Gables
Alice in Wonderland becomes Alice of Wonderland

The Three Sisters—style, form and content

According to Iroquois legend, corn, beans, and squash are three inseparable sisters who only grow and thrive together. This tradition of interplanting corn, beans and squash in the same mounds, widespread among Native American farming societies, is a sophisticated, sustainable system that provided long-term soil fertility and a healthy diet to generations. Growing a Three Sisters garden is a wonderful way to feel more connected to the history of this land, regardless of our ancestry.

Style

"...all the work is in the style ..."
        Susan Sontag

...from the poet John B. Lee's December 6/05 letter

Dear John Porter

I've finally cleared the decks and am reading your wonderful, thought-provoking love letter to the written word, your book, Spirit Book Word.

If one agrees with Susan Sontag's belief that in writing "all the work is in the style", this is a masterful achievement.

"I want a quiet voice, a little voice, a whisper, for I'm telling you a secret I'm not quite sure of myself. A secret I can spoil by a wrongful telling. Will you listen? I have a story to tell—a story of my relationship with ten words and the writers who bring them to flesh, a story of my stutter to pronounce my own lifeword."
   John Porter, from Spirit Book Word

This is wonderful writing, John. I was reading it in the hottub, a place where I float my belly and call myself, "a hottub Buddha". I lingered. Read. Re-read. Savoured. Thought. Read again. Read by slow exhales and taking in of breaths. Wished I'd written such words. Had such thoughts. Said such things.

I'm brought to remember James Reaney's talk at the Visionary conference in Guelph, where he unashamedly and enthusiastically said this simple thing, "I love stories." He said it deep. We were in a church sitting in pews gathered together for a conference on the visionary tradition in Canadian literature. Poets, novelists, essayist, professors, people who believe in the transformative power of poetry and story. How the best words in the best order might change a person's inner life.

I also think of Stan Dragland's books, Journey Through Bookland, and The Bees of the Invisibile, the title based on Rilke's letter.

You've got me thinking about my own 'spirit words.' I confess, I love too many words to settle upon a single one. And I'm not certain I'm far enough along on the journey of the soul to know what my spirit word might be. Perhaps it might be "home."

Email by John B. Lee sent to John Porter after reading Porter's book Spirit Book Word

When I think of the craft of writing, I think of the three essential elements of every work of literature. I think of style, form and content. And just as the Iroquois legend sees in the three sisters of agriculture complementary and sustaining features of corn, beans and squash, I contend that the three complementary and sustaining features of all works of literature in general and of poetry in particular are style, form and content. Let me begin by iterating what I mean when I use the word style.

Style in writing involves word choice and word order. The individual nature of style as it varies from author to author is what I would call voice. And sometimes, a great writer might be an author of a multitude of voices. And sometimes, when the author throws his voice beyond the range of his or her individual voice, the author might say of his own voice, as I claimed in the voice of one poem, "I am many voices not my own." The hen clucks, the rooster crows, the dog barks, whines, yaps, and growls, the goose honks and the owls hoot, in my lexicon, my dictionary, my English. How do you say woof in Spanish—guau? Does the hen ever cocadoodledoo?

Does the gull quack? The voice of the poem should be true to the voice of the experience of the poem. The voice/style of the poem should also be in harmony with the point of view, or if not in harmony with the point of view, at least sensibly connected. Think here of the phrase the eloquent redneck, or the difference between solemnity and seriousness. Something very important can also be seriously silly. And its importance need not be undermined by silliness. Solemnity can be deadly.

I think here of the woof and the wag, the cluck and the peck, the snap and the slither, the growl and bite of the language we choose. Bedwetting is understandable in babies and the incontinent few, but in the after-thinker's final analysis and for the reader's sake, the outpouring of which I have written is no longer cute when the reader receives the work. The energy of spill and splash when it's wild on the trousers, wild on the kitchen floor or wild in the wilderness snow is very different and we all know the difference. We know the difference between being Solomon and being Sirius. The one is a wise king, the other a dog star. We all share the same dictionary. In the dictionary music of poetry and in the voice of the individual poet we have evidence that songbirds do indeed dream of their songs in their sleep. And the finch is not a dove, the crow is not a whippoorwill.

Form

"You say that I pay too much attention to form. Alas! it is like body and soul: form and content to me are one: I

don't know what either is without the other."
Gustave Flaubert in a letter

By form I mean the organizing structure of the piece of writing or what we sometimes call the genre of the writing. In literature class I learned the word mode in isolating and describing the different voices involved in writing. There were the poetic, the narrative, the dramatic, the expository, and the presentational mode. Within the traditions of poetry there are an almost limitless number of modes or forms. The lyric and the narrative voice in poetry are often blent within the same poem. The entire cataloguing and explication of these varieties of forms and voices are far too broad and capacious and profoundly intermixed to explore in any meaningful way in this book. Suffice it to say — go to the library, read every book there, read it as a writer reads, when you come to know, you'll know that you know. Let me simply provide a few examples and then send you to the library to do the work, the lifelong work of reading and expanding and deepening your understanding of the inherited traditions of voice and form.

I was once asked by a friend to explain the difference between doggerel and serious verse. This is very difficult to do when the person asking the question values certain popular practitioners of light verse especially when that person is incapable of distinguishing between description of type and criticism of type. He was inquiring about his own personal favourite poet, the very popular Canadian poet Robert Service beloved author of "The Shooting of Dan McGrew," and "The

Cremation of Sam McGee." He asked me point-blank to tell him why Service is not considered an important poet by the elitists who exclude him from anthologies of serious poetry by major poets.

In responding to his question I pointed out the twin features of easy rhyme and facile rhythm that are the hallmarks of almost all the canon of light verse. The two aforementioned poems are melodramatic rather than dramatic. The personalities in them are caricatures rather than characters. The former poem involves romantic love, illicit sex, gunplay and murder. The latter poem belongs to the elegiac tradition. However, if it is something of a lamentation of loss, the metaphysics are those worthy of cartoon great Bugs Bunny and the lamentation is that of a dog in a barn mourning his state. Of course, the fan of Service missing my point entirely took offence, called me an elitist and a snob. This same individual also fails to distinguish between Service, who is essentially a master of doggerel, and Edgar Allan Poe or Henry Wadsworth Longfellow whose works are easily ridiculed because their form and style are out of fashion. A contemporary reader quickly tires of the clip clop rhythms of Longfellow's masterpiece *The Song of Hiawatha*, or Poe's poem, "The Raven." Read the opening lines of Longfellow's poem:

> Should you ask me, whence these stories?
> Whence these legends and traditions,
> With the odors of the forest,
> With the dew and damp of meadows,
> With the curling smoke of wigwams,

With the rushing of the rivers,
With their frequent repetitions,
And their wild reverberations,
As of thunder in the mountains?
I should answer, I should tell you,
"From the forest and the prairies,
From the great lakes of the Northland,
From the land of the Ojibways,
From the land of the Dacotahs,
From the mountains, moors, and fen-lands
Where the heron, the Shuh-shuh-gah,
Feeds among the rushes.

Anyone of refined taste and reliable judgment soon realizes the undeniable quality of the work, but the reader also acknowledges that this form and style are so out of fashion as to seem to trivialize the content. I call the failure to recognize the reader/responder's predilection to appreciate old-verse techniques in contemporary poetry, putting the top hat on the tiger.

Frost's lovely verse, "Stopping by Woods on a Snowy Evening," does not fall hard on the end rhyme, and the quality of its meter is entirely complementary to both its tone and its content. And so, Robert Frost remains readable to a contemporary reader who would find Longfellow's formalism quaint. Consider Pope's rhyming couplet compared with American neo-formalist A. R. Ammons use of the couplet. The form one chooses is almost always chosen by an intuitive understanding of the relationship between the content of the poem and the impact of the form. One learns this relationship from the inside out and from the outside in. The writer reads, observes and responds in a reliable way to the received object, the well-written poem. The writer also practices the craft and notices what works, when it works, how it works and either through intuition or observation and analysis comes to know. The authentic poem choses the form it wishes to set up house in.

When asked to define jazz Louis Armstrong is said to have responded, "If you gotta ask, you'll never know." As for me, I'd suggest, if you don't know yet, go to the library, read until you know what I mean by style, form and content. And then you'll know.

Content

What I mean by content is the experience a reader might have by reading a piece of literature and thereby recreating the experience present in the language inspired by the original experience of the poet. It is for each author to discover for himself or herself what stories he or she has been given to tell. Publisher Marty Gervais is one of the most profoundly gifted men with the capacity to know exactly what a writer should be writing about. He inspired Mary Ann Mulhern to write about her life as a young woman who gave her life for a time to the convent. He inspired Terry Ann Carter to write about her mentally ill brother's disappearance. He demanded that I write a memoir of my life growing up on the farm. He intuits the central story of your life. He knows your authentic story. The one you were born to write.

I once put it this way: "Write what you know about; know what you write about. Write what you care about; care what you write about." If you don't care about the sky, don't write about the sky. The results of such writing, however inspired, however much of a tour de force, however much the product of a profoundly crafted author, the work will always be lacking.

The best poems I have ever written, and I daresay the best poems you will ever write will be those poems where the content is so compelling it insists upon coming to life, the form is so absolutely appropriate, it matches the content like the veil that clings to the contours of the body in a gentle breeze, and the style is the voice of the rabbit in the body of the hare. Just as the god of a goose is a goose and the god of a gull, a gull, so too the perfect poem is the one you are about to write. It wills itself alive in the breath of your ink. The dictionary music leaps onto the page and you must rush to keep pace.

And Furthermore

Where Do I Write: the boy who made his own desk

One of the questions that students of writing frequently ask me is, "Where do you write?" And I always say, "When I write, I want to be alone in a room, alone in the house, alone on the street, alone in the town, alone in the nation, alone in the world, and alone in the universe." In other words, I seek sublime solitude. And ever since I have lived away from the home of my birth on the farm, I have managed to achieve the luxury of having a study in which to seek and find solitude and a writing desk on which to compose my thoughts.

And although I had a bedroom of my own on the farm, I did not have a desk. When I realized at about twelve years of age that I secretly wanted to be a writer, I begged my father to buy me a desk on which to write. That didn't happen. Somehow, since he hadn't bought me a bicycle either, nor did he buy me a bed, I knew that a writing desk was an unlikely prospect.

The first bike I ever rode was a shocking pink girl's bike left on the farm by cousin Helen. I learned how to ride on that bike, but when my grandfather Busteed saw me riding a pink bike, he said, "the boy needs a man's bike," and so he brought from his shed an old man's bike two sizes too big for me. I fastened longhorn handlebars on the front, fixed a banana seat to the frame and rode high on the gravel like a gentleman on a penny-farthing. I'd slept in a crib until one day when I was five, my grandfather Busteed said, "that boy needs a bed," and so I acquired the bed I would sleep in for the next ten years.

However, despite my expectations for disappointment, when the clerk's table came up for auction in the village, my father proudly struck a bargain, bought it, and brought it home for me. Unfortunately, it was a table designed for writing while standing up, or perhaps one might imagine the clerk sitting on a high stool ciphering the books for the next council audit. It seemed Dickensian enough, something Bartleby the Scrivener might use, but I didn't fancy myself dipping my quill in a well and squinting over columns of numbers. I wanted a poet's writing desk. Something Hemingway might own. And so, I grabbed a dull handsaw from the barn and sawed two feet off each of the four legs. From then on, it wobbled like cottage card table and it did not satisfy. In addition to being cocked by my bad carpentry, the top was canted to serve nineteenth century stand-up ergonomics.

Then I had an idea. I'd make my own student's writing desk. I found a two-foot by four-foot sheet of plywood from the barn. I think it might have been meant for a pig partition. I sawed off two one by one's for legs and found two orange crates and stood them side by each, on end. I hammered in six ten penny nails, sanded and varnished the top, and "voila" I had my first writing desk. And there I wrote my early poems. The first poem I ever had published, "Thoughts of a Mouse at High Tide," was written there, and a poem I still think of as a keeper, "My Alibi for an Eventful Wednesday in May," was written there when I was an aspiring seventeen-year-old high school poet.

Now, I write on a manufactured desk. Alone at my study window, I compose my poems, but I have a photograph of that first scrivener's station, that ideal writing locale, the one I hammered together with things I'd found at the barn on the farm, the desk my father wouldn't buy me, the desk I had to make on my own. I use that photograph as my screen saver, and it reminds me of my younger self, the lad who aspired to be a poet, that boy who made his own desk from orange crates and plywood and six ten-penny dreams.

A Poet's Voice: author's statement

Poetry slows us down; requires that we linger in the moment, and that we are attentive to that which deepens experience. If we might accept the truth of Marianne Moore's statement that "poetry is imaginary gardens with real toads in them," and if we might agree with Coleridge's definition that poetry is "the best words in the best order," and if we might know what MacLeish meant in his wonderful poem, "Ars poetica," when he wrote "poems should not mean/But be," and we might feel hairs on the nape of the neck rising when the words sing, then we have it in us to partake in magical thinking and we might find in dictionary music the connection between the deep wells of the self and the far realms of the universe, between the indwelling soul and the all-encompassing spirit. I want the best poems to challenge the mind, to touch the heart, to thrill the body, to enthrall the soul, and to include the spirit in one surround.

From "Humanist Perspectives," Summer 2011, Issue 177

The muses and me

What I seek to achieve in writing a poem is a profound connection with the deeper wells of myself, and to vanish into the work and into the world. I chase the feeling I feel when the work is going well. What it requires of me is that I be entirely absent, that I disappear. Ideally, I am alone in a room, alone in the house, alone on the street, alone in the city, alone in the universe. To accomplish that, I mostly write in isolation, in my study, surrounded by books and images, sitting at my desk, in front of my window, only rarely catching a glimpse of what is occurring in the yard, and thereby catching the words in flight. I tend to work very quickly. I rarely change a line. I rush my lead to keep up with my mind. I seek those moments when the heart, the mind, the body and the soul are contained in one surround. I refuse to doubt what I'm doing while I'm working. Then, in the cruel light of the after-thinker, I reject the poems that seem unworthy of a stranger's attention. The keepers, I type out and place in a manuscript. They gather like leaves in late autumn. I shape them into what I think are meaningful juxtapositions of new cross-fertilizing and cumulative meaning. I make from them books, sometimes eclectic, sometimes connected by more than the accidental proximity of time. Most recently, the manuscript, *How Beautiful We Are*, which won the inaugural Orison/Souwesto Writing Award, has Port Dover as its inspiration; *Godspeed* is inspired by the life and times of Bartholomew Gosnold, founder of Jamestown; and *Being Human* is purely serendipitous accumulation shaped by careful arrangement. I'm now thinking of a new gathering called, *The Widow's Land*. I haven't written much yet; however, I am flooding the breakwall of anticipation. I write because I love to write. I am indeed a fortunate.

From 'Centred Out' featured in the magazine Hammered Out

No Such Place As Nowhere

"...so far from anywhere
even homing pigeons lost their way
getting back home to nowhere
we built a house* so flagrantly noticeable
it seemed an act of despair..."
           from In Search of Own Roblin, by Al Purdy

Like Al Purdy, it sometimes seemed as I grew up that I too resided in the exact middle of nowhere. My father's farm, the farm on the hill he called home, is located somewhere between no place called Highgate and some place called someplace else. I recall those elementary school days, when wishing to get a fix on private geography, we wrote of ourselves as situated on a list leading from the banal particularity of a postal address radiating outward from drab village to dull township, to bland county, to parochial province, to boring nation, to familiar continent, to known hemisphere, to home planet, to occupied solar system marked for motion by the orrery at school placing ourselves in orbit within the milky swirl of the local galaxies and from there to the ever-expansive impossibly-distant membranous edge at the outer reaches the universe—infinity and beyond to the very extra-temporal extra-spatial mind of God.

My incarnation conceived in a rural farmhouse, born in a small-city hospital, nursed in a bucolic cradle, nurtured two years too long in a jail-sided crib, came of age in a double-bed bedroom at the top of the stairs to the south of the house built before my father was born. In that same room, my ancestors slept away their plaster-ceiling youth. In that same room, my father and then my aunt and her daughter fought the skittering of midnight mice to steal a quiet dream. The solitary window opened onto a lawn leading down to a garden, and from there, across cow pasture to the back fields where the railway ran from Chicago in the west to Buffalo in the east and beyond. The four brave perimeters of those two hundred family acres defined and confined my world for the first seventeen years of my life. Like most imaginative children I dreamed of escape and the adventure available only elsewhere than here. The road in the north known as the Gosnell line ended a mile away in the village where I attended elementary school during the week and went to the Anglican Church on Sundays. In summers we rode the wagon to work at the farm known as the Other Place. The road lead to the west and from there to the small town of Ridgetown where I attended high school and in English class did not study the poets of my region nor did I study the poets of my nation.

I did not study Archibald Lampman who was raised in nearby Morpeth. I did not study Raymond Knister Canada's first modernist poet, who convalesced on his father's Cedar Springs peach farm while he wrote poems and stories set in the rural landscape near Blenheim of the 1920's, the decade of my mother's birth in Mull mere miles away. I did not study James Reaney who was raised on a farm near Stratford and who popularized the word Souwesto, a word that strove to give legitimacy and importance to my region. And I did not study Margaret Avison, Irving Layton, Al Purdy or any of the number of Canadian poets of a generation who might have given credence to the possibility that I lived somewhere worthy of my own attention. But when as a young adult I discovered their work I woke to the possibility that I lived an interesting life set in a fascinating geography.

First awakened by four Liverpool lads and then by a Swansea poet whose Fern Hill childhood gave apple-bough comfort to my own rural youth, I fell asleep with Byron bird-winged on my breast. Before my poets left behind an old romance, cut their hair and hung their red vests on a post, I learned to come alive in my body to the words that gave my language authority and hope. Finally, I wrote about the farm without shame. The earth that gave my feet the gift of local gravity set Homer on the shoulder of a local furrow and on the crest of curling under combers of my lake. Why not imagine Achilles born as he was in the mind of Knister dreaming of Troy as he broke corn ground with the Iliad in his hip pocket walking the flat-field acres of his father's home farm. Why not imagine Milton's Lucifer lost in the turning soil of James Reaney raised on a crooked road near Stratford. Why not think of Purdy hopping the rails and riding with D.H. Lawrence lifting his eyes from the land. What gives the country North of Bellville a better reason to be than that? To have someone live there who honours existence by writing the place into life. After all, New York, London, Paris, these too are nowhere in particular when the mind and soul of the resident die into the dullness of a ho-hum existence.

Every life is interesting. Every place is somewhere. This is what we know when we have the good fortune to live in the presence of writers who are fully awake and fully alive in their world.

Near the end of his life, just such a writer—Al Purdy— and I struck up a correspondence. I wrote him requesting original new writing for two anthologies on which I was working at the time. He proved to be quite open and generous and I acquired a poem for one of the anthologies. Our correspondence ended up appearing in the posthumously published letters of Al Purdy. The poem he sent me appears in the Black Moss Press anthology, *I Want to Be the Poet of Your Kneecaps*. I have no way of knowing for certain, but I believe it may be the last poem Al Purdy wrote before descending into the final illness from which he would not emerge. He had been sick for a while with influenza when a young man believing himself to be the illegitimate son of Gwendolyn MacEwen visited him. We had a good laugh over the subject matter of the poem and indeed the humorous treatment therein of mortality remains a profound irony given the fact that Purdy only a few weeks after sending the poem became mortally ill.

Peoples' Poetry and the Fallacy of Accessibility

People want poetry that connects them to life.

Whenever I write at my best, in addition to chasing the feeling I feel when the writing is going well, I also aspire to achieve a profound connection to the deepest wells of the self. And in so doing, and whenever I accomplish that difficult magic, I hope through and by way of the poem to make a similar connection with and for the reader/re-creator whom I assume to be a living stranger, fully awake, fully alive, curious and hungry for shared experience who comes to the cold dead ink of the page prepared to revivify original experience by plunging inward and allowing to radiate outward the original impulse and the subsequent result of that creative event.

People's poetry honours this connection between poet and poem, poem and reader, by celebrating learning, preserving memory, daring to imagine, attending to language, thinking deeply and feeling profoundly about being fully awake and fully alive in the centre of life. When it is born in the world, to those who live in the world it joins the common man with the learnèd man, inviting them both to roll up their sleeves and gather together in a fields. I think here of John Updike's poem on hoeing. When it is born in the library and lives most comfortably within institutions of learning, it invites a sharing of knowledge with those who live beyond the shadow of erudition and formal education. I think here of Eliot's *Waste Land* or of the other metaphysical poets of modernism. If there is complexity, it exists is service of deeper meaning. Though deep wells may indeed be dark, we need not assume they are not clear. It only wants the presence of light to prove transparency. Sometimes that light is a light we carry such as the light of learning, sometimes the light comes from within the dim regions of the darkness of the individual reader. And the best poems long to reveal themselves in their greatest depths as limpid and pure. Never either needlessly obscure nor obviously difficult, they may slow us down and make us linger a while, but when we look well we see, when we listen closely we hear, when we invite engagement we feel the poem in the flesh, we know it in the mind, it thrills the body and feeds the soul. We are not kept out by a private club of academics, nor are we are excluded by a secret society of like-minded elitists.

Manuel

In my aspiration as a writer I wish to write "the smell of varnish". In this intention, it is language that fails the author. Canadian poet bp Nichol wrote, "I do not wish to write a poem about a daffodil, I want to write a poem which is a daffodil."

In writing, I want the poem to have the transformative power of prayer. Most people think of prayer as an importuning of God. I think of it as an appeal from the inner world of the individual to the outer world of the universe to make a connection whereby the iteration of the best words in the best order presents the possibility of grace, the covenant between the self and the universe, the vanishing into the thing where the soul makes contact through the mind, the body, the heart with the enthralling and all-containing spirit of things. Existence without alienation. What the authors of the Bible meant when they spoke of the covenant between God and man for which the rainbow is a metaphor.

It is this luminous interior connecting with this 'startlingly brilliant sky', this egoless dark, this close-eyed heaven we hold, that I'm after in my work. And why would my aspiration as a translator be any less ambitious. To prove the original stamp in the copy, that is my hope. To find in my language, the shadow of light in the ink of the primary text, like saying in echoes as close to the source of original voice without losing the voice of the source.

Oh how the original cried out in its mask.

And when the mask is removed, what face is there to be seen.

Imagine the bones of the poem invisible.

Imagine translating back from the translation and attempting to achieve the original.

And this is in the same language where the culture and the intention of the original poem is entirely understood.

What a job we have taken on in attempting to honour these poets and these poems.

*

These poets in exile, these poets suffering under the yoke of the imperial tyranny of Spain, these poets as soldiers in a battle fighting to realize Cuban independence, these poets living and dying and lamenting the tragic loss of lovers and friends, these poets who never lose faith in the possibility of the establishment of a human paradise worthy of the natural beauty of their beloved island, many of them martyrs to that cause, many of them perishing without realizing this ideal in their lifetime, this aspiration given voice by many and culminating in Martí and evolving from his dream into the dream of those who inherited his ideal, this is the voice of *Sweet Cuba*, this bitter-sweet beauty in the lingual music of poetry manifest in the two-tongued poems of this anthology.

I feel a deep connection to Cuba that I hope to live to deserve.

January 20, 2012 from "Afterward: Translating from the English—Finding Voice" first published in Sweet Cuba: The Building of a Poetic Tradition: 1608-1958 (Hidden Brook Press, 2010)

Even at the Worst of Times

"Even at the worst of times, writing poems has been joyous and rewarding."
  Al Purdy from "To See the Shore"

The very first poems I ever wrote, thinking I might some day become a poet, were bad in every sense of the word but one — I did not know how bad they were. They were bad beyond the know of bad. But they were always a pleasure to write. And that pleasure in writing remains with me even to this day. Whenever I am writing I am chasing the feeling I feel arising from the thrill of writing when the writing is going well.

I got started learning the craft so long to learn the moment I saw the Beatles on television. The very next morning I woke up as if reborn, and I wrote to honour John, Paul, George and Ringo. I wanted their attention. I wrote in the full-blush of my badness and then when I overheard my sister reading those poems on the phone to her boyfriend saying something about her brother being a poet and I almost believed her. I showed my poems to my mother who showed them to my father saying, "You should pay attention to what your son is doing." I showed poems to friends who shared a preteen enthusiasm for those four guys from England and I basked for a time in the pallid light of their praise. Of course it wasn't long before I outgrew the lad who thought he was good at making poems. Fortunately, I grew into the lad who yearned to honour the achievements of poets who came before. I aspired to make poems wherein the language I used served a larger truth than the one I knew as John. At the same time I wanted to capture what my world was like to me. I desired to know death, eternity, and the secret mysteries of sex.

This new and more reliable self came into being the day I first read "Fern Hill." That poem taught me what could be done when the poem connects the reader to life. I did not know it then, but I was beginning my journey as a writer writing in a tradition that has been called People's Poetry in England and Canada and Populist Poetry in the United States of America.

While still in high school I wrote hundreds of poems, all of them a joy to create, all of them brilliant in the moment and awful in a week. And then in May of my eighteenth year I wrote my first keeper, "My Alibi for an Eventful Wednesday in May". I knew it was the real thing when I still liked it a week, and then in a month, and then in a year after it was first conceived. And I still like it in the here and now. There are qualities in that poem which I seek to recapture with every poem I write.

And the tradition to which I belong, though sometimes called accessible, requires more than learning and mere intelligence. The brain flickers in dull gloom when we rely upon intelligence alone. A clever and insipid irony all too often masquerades as brilliance shining in shallow mud. Mere language play and a busy head, the trickery of a lively performance, the paltry illusion of a complex game, the easy rhyme and facile rhythm of popular verse, each might receive the attention and briefly excite the admiration of an applauding crowd, but when the dust settles the crowd soon forgets.

I want, in poems, for the heart to feel true sentiment, the head to know eternal truth, the body to come alive with full-fleshed bone-buzzing experience, the soul to thrill to a commingling of temporal and extra-temporal things, and the spirit to surround and be surrounded by an interplay between the deep wells of the self and the stars beyond the farthest stars we might dream but never see. I want the past alive, the present reified and the future remembered in words so perfect they sing alone and in chorus the name of names. I also know that deep wells though dark might indeed be clear. It only wants a sure and reliable light. A great poem might be that light made available.

Originally published in And Left a Place Too Stand On: poems and essays on Al Purdy (Hidden Brook Press, 2009)

Wishful Thinking: dear Manuel

from an email by John B. Lee

Recently, Christopher Hitchens died of cancer. His was a fine mind and he was a major voice in the neo-atheistic movement taken root in the secular age here in the privileged democracies of the west.

From my point of view, he over-values the rational mind and gives far too much credit to the scientific method and to science as a body of knowledge.

A close friend of mine, during a discussion concerning religion and what he perceives as the neurosis of faith said, "A belief in God and in the consolation of an afterlife is just wishful thinking," to which I replied, "What is wrong with wishful thinking?"

To me, faith is only truly faith, if it includes DOUBT. Otherwise, faith becomes absolute, righteousness becomes self-righteousness, and piety becomes sanctimony.

You may recall that in one poem from my collection *But Where Were the Horses of Evening*, I wrote, "my God does not even believe in Himself."

This is the tragic ipseity that leads to the creation of man, making mankind the God affirmation. God created man as an affirmation of His own self-awareness. "I am that I am" is solipsistic, and the need to create a mortal reflection, a dying companion completes an otherwise incomplete immortality with its need for otherness.

We humans are lonesome creatures. We crave companionship, and in so doing, we know ourselves as reified by that which is other.

The empty mirror still reflects the room. It is the "seeing" that creates the seen thing.

American critic Harold Bloom speaks of Christ as a mortal god, and man as an immortal animal. This is the story of our relationship with the outer world and the inner self.

The primary world is made meaningful by the secondary reification in the mind of man. We sense a deep connection between the inner self and the natural world, even as far as the farthest star beyond our imagining.

In the story of Eden, (and this gave rise to my thoughts concerning the title I suggested for our anthology *Beyond the Seventh Morning*), I have the sense of a Creator whose work is complete, and in this completion I feel the great tragedy of that accomplishment involving a "now what?" and that sense of God's great sorrow gave rise to a line I wrote when I was very young, "the tragic ipseity of creation's overness."

How sad to think of God, His work complete, setting in motion this clockwork universe where all things are known and pre-ordained. Like a child watching a toy train go round and round and round and round in a never-ending circle on the basement floor of a Christmas morning. How soon ennui would set in. How the child prays for the train wreck managed by his little dog, or a hotbox event. The need to intervene, to change the route, to IMAGINE it differently.

So, here is my theory concerning the relationship between the Creator and Man. We ARE the mischief, the creature created who amuses, pleases, frustrates, angers, delights, worships, and disappoints the Creator.

That old conundrum, "If God is all powerful, then surely he might be able to create a stone too heavy for even Him to lift."

The mischief of PARADOX. The tragedy of IRONY. These elements of story highlight one reason why The Bible remains a great story central to our predicament. We are trapped, our souls tied to a dying animal. We aspire to and are inspired by our self-delighting limitations. Einstein once wrote, "the most incomprehensible thing about the universe is the fact that it is comprehensible." This tautology requires a fine imagination.

American poet, Donald Hall visited world-renowned sculptor Henry Moore, when Hall was a young man and Moore an elder of the tribe. When Hall asked Moore the secret of the great artist's life, Moore said to his young admirer, "The secret of life is to have a task, something you devote your entire life to, something you bring everything to, every minute of every day for your whole life. And the most important thing is — it must be something you cannot possibly do."

So, as for God, and Christ, and the sources of story that predate the scriptures: the Beatitudes are anticipated by Egyptian texts; the story of creation in Genesis has its parallel in the Greek myth of Prometheus; the tale of the flood exists in Gilgamesh, (a much older document than the Mosaic Pentateuch); the story of Christ has its progenitor in the Egyptian god Horus, and there is much evidence in the post Nietzschean deicide of recent secular humanist trends in western societies, that have their parallel in the decline of the Roman gods, even as Ovid was immortalizing them in story during the reign of Augustus and the years surrounding the birth of Christ.

To all of this, I say, "SO WHAT!"

American poet Emily Dickinson wrote, "And then a Plank of Reason broke,/ And I dropped down and down—/ and struck a world at every plunge ..."

I happily embrace a belief in God, if by God we mean the better self, the one consoled by story. I believe in story. The better the story, the deeper the experience, the more profound the possibility of grace.

I refuse to allow the theft of joy that comes from being diminished by an alienating solitude. This selfsame solitude presents the greatest possibility of community, belonging, a sort of enlightened solitude, a luminous aloneness. Only when I'm alone am I truly present with the radiant possibility of universal connection. Here I sit, at this machine, and you are with me, my friend, a thousand miles away in Cuba, and though my wife sits in the other room, still we are ONE. We vanish into the possibility of deeper presence.

When we pray, when we create, when we love and are loved, then we glimpse the transformative possibility of the selfless self, the soul in us shines, and we feel the covenant with God, the universe and all.

The mirror in the empty room shows the room the vacant desire to be seen beyond the seventh morning.

Acknowledgements

"A Poet's Voice" first appeared in the *HumanPerspectives* magazine

"Where Do I Write" first appeared on Marty Gervais' web site

"The Muses and Me" first appeared in *Hammered Out*

"Manuel" first appeared in *Sweet Cuba: The Building of a Poetic Tradition*

"Even at the Worst of Times" first appeared in *And Left A Place to Stand On: poems and essays on Al Purdy*

"Wishful Thinking" first appeared in *Beyond the Seventh Morning*

Author

In 2005 John B. Lee was inducted as Poet Laureate of Brantford in perpetuity and in 2011 he was appointed Poet Laureate of Norfolk County. The same year he received the distinction of being named Honourary Life Member of The Canadian Poetry Association. In 2007 he was made a member of the Chancellor's Circle of the President's Club of McMaster University and he was named winner of the inaugural Black Moss Press Souwesto Award for his contribution to the ethos of writing in Southwestern Ontario. A recipient of over sixty prestigious international awards for his writing, he is winner of the $10,000 CBC Literary Award for Poetry, the only two time recipient of the People's Poetry Award, and 2006 winner of the inaugural Souwesto/Orison Writing Award (University of Windsor). In 2007 he was named winner of the Winston Collins Award for Best Canadian Poem and in 2010 he received the Award of Merit for Professional Achievement presented by the University of Western Ontario and The International Poets Academy Lifetime Achievement Award for his contribution to Peace through Poetry. He has well-over fifty books published to date and is the editor of eleven anthologies including two best-selling works: That Sign of Perfection: poems and stories on the game of hockey; and Smaller Than God: words of spiritual longing. His work has appeared internationally in over 500 publications, and has been translated into French, Spanish, Korean and Chinese. He has read his work in nations all over the world including South Africa, France, Korea, Cuba, Canada and the United States. He has received letters of praise from Nelson Mandela, Desmond Tutu, Australian Poet, Les Murray, and Senator Romeo Dallaire. Called "the greatest living poet in English," by poet George Whipple, he lives with his wife Cathy in Port Dover, Ontario where he works as a full time author.

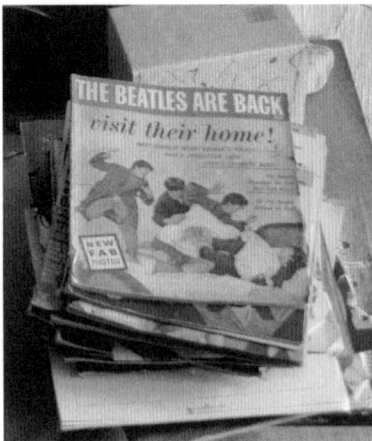